Bright Line Eating Cookbook

Quick and Easy

Bright Line Eating Recipes for

Your Whole Health

Missy Armstrong

EASY GARBANZO BEAN SALAD
SERVING SIZE: 1
SERVINGS PER RECIPE: 4
CALORIES: 233
COOKING TIME: 1 HOUR

INGREDIENTS:
Lemons—3
Olive oil—2 tablespoons
Garlic—1 tablespoon, minced
Cucumber—1, small, chopped
Red onion—½, small, chopped
Cherry tomatoes—1 cup, halved
Chickpeas—1 can, 19 ounces, drained and rinsed
Salt—to taste
Pepper—to taste
Fresh parsley—2 tablespoons, chopped

NUTRITION INFORMATION:

Carbohydrate—44 g

Protein—34 g

Fat—12 g

Sodium—357 mg

Cholesterol—56 mg

INSTRUCTIONS:

1. Take a serving bowl and squeeze the three lemons in it. Add olive oil to the lemon juice and also add the minced garlic.

2. Put the red onion, chickpeas, cucumber, and cherry tomatoes in the bowl and stir well. Sprinkle salt and pepper to taste. Combine well.

3. Sprinkle chopped fresh parsley on top of it to garnish.

4. Allow it to refrigerate for about an hour before serving.

5. Your dish is ready to be served.

VEGETABLE CURRY IN INDIAN STYLE

SERVING SIZE: 1 ¼ CUPS
SERVINGS PER RECIPE: 4
CALORIES: 145
COOKING TIME: 25 MINUTES

INGREDIENTS:

Onion—1, small, chopped
Garlic cloves—4, roughly chopped
Jalapeno pepper—1, seeded, chopped
Water—2 tablespoons
Canola oil—1 tablespoon
Sweet curry powder—2 tablespoons
Sweet potato—1, peeled, cut into 1-inch chunks
Carrots—2, peeled, cut into 1-inch chunks
Red bell pepper—1, seeded, cut into 1-inch chunks
Fresh green beans—6 ounces, trimmed, halves
Green onion—4, thinly sliced
Unsweetened coconut milk—½ cups
Vegetable broth—1 cup, low sodium
Cornstarch—1 tablespoon
Cilantro—2 tablespoons, chopped
Paprika—1 teaspoon
Salt—½ teaspoon, optional
Black pepper—¼ teaspoon

NUTRITION INFORMATION:

Carbohydrate—24 g
Protein—3 g
Fat—5 g
Sodium—75 mg
Cholesterol—0 mg

INSTRUCTIONS:

1. Take a blender and add garlic, onion, jalapeno, and water in it. Puree it to make a paste.

2. In a large saucepan, add oil and let it heat over high heat. Now add the onion paste along with the curry powder in the oil and allow it to sauté for another 4 minutes. Keep stirring frequently.

3. Now add the sweet potatoes and also the carrots in the paste. Sauté it for another 4 minutes and stir well.

4. Put the green beans, red bell pepper, and scallions in it and sauté for about 2 minutes.

5. Take a small bowl and add the vegetable broth, coconut milk, and cornstarch in it. Whisk it well. Now pour this mixture over the vegetables. Bring it to a boil. Reduce the heat and allow it to simmer for about 10 minutes, covered.

6. Sprinkle salt and black pepper as desired. Also, add the cilantro and paprika in it.

7. Your vegetable curry is ready to be served.

SUSHI BOWLS WITH SRIRACHA MAYO

SERVING SIZE: 1 BOWL
SERVINGS PER RECIPE: 4
CALORIES: 563
COOKING TIME: 30 MINUTES

INGREDIENTS:

FOR SUSHI RICE:

   White grain rice—2 cups
   Water—2 cups
   Rice vinegar—2 tablespoons
   White sugar—2 tablespoons
   Salt—1 teaspoon

FOR TOPPINGS:

   Crabstick—4 ounces
   Carrot—1
   Cucumber—1
   Avocado—1
   Nori snack pack—1
   Sesame seeds—1 tablespoon

FOR SRIRACHA MAYO:

   Mayonnaise—4 tablespoons
   Sriracha—2 tablespoons

NUTRITION INFORMATION:

   Carbohydrate—34 g
   Protein –22 g
   Fat—16 g
   Sodium—459 mg
   Cholesterol –87 mg

INSTRUCTIONS:

1. Take a medium sauté pot and put the medium-short grain rice in it. Cover the rice with cool water. Turn the rice around in the water for about 3–4 times to rinse off the uncooked rice well. Strain the rinsed water and add 2 cups of the freshwater for cooking. Close the lid of the pot and put it over high heat. Bring it to a boil. Reduce the heat to low and allow it to simmer for about 15 minutes. Turn the heat off and allow the rice to rest for about 10 minutes, undisturbed.

2. To prepare the toppings, shred the crabstick well, slice the cucumber and avocado, julienne the carrot, and break the Nori into tiny pieces.

3. In a small bowl, add the mayonnaise and Sriracha in it. Stir well.

4. To make the sushi rice dressing, take a small bowl and add sugar, rice vinegar, and salt in it. Microwave it for about 15–20 seconds and stir well until the sugar is fully dissolved.

5. Transfer the rice to a large bowl. Sprinkle 1/4th of the vinegar dressing on top of the rice and gently fold the rice well. Repeat the process with the remaining vinegar dressing until the rice has a glossy appearance.

6. To prepare the sushi bowls, take a bowl and add about 1 cup of the sushi rice in it. Top it with carrot, cucumber, crabstick, avocado, and Nori. Also, add a pinch of the sesame seeds. Now drizzle the Sriracha mayo over the sushi bowl.

7. Your dish is ready to be served.

GRILLED STEAK WITH FRESH MANGO SALSA

SERVING SIZE: 3 OUNCES OF STEAK WITH 1/4TH CUP OF SALSA
SERVINGS PER RECIPE: 4
CALORIES: 223
COOKING TIME: 25 MINUTES

INGREDIENTS:

Garam masala—1 teaspoon
Brown sugar—1 teaspoon
Salt—1/4th teaspoon
Black pepper—½ teaspoon, freshly ground
Flank steak—1 pound
Fresh mango—1 cup, peeled, diced
Cucumber—¼ cup, seeded, diced
Fresh cilantro—1 tablespoon, chopped
Fresh lime juice—1 tablespoon
Fresh ginger—¼ teaspoon, peeled, minced
Salt—to taste

NUTRITION INFORMATION:

Carbohydrate—8.6 g
Protein—21.5 g
Fat—11.1 g
Sodium—251 mg
Cholesterol—71 mg

INSTRUCTIONS:

1. Preheat the grill to a temperature of medium-high heat.

2. Mix the garam masala, brown sugar, salt, and black pepper together in a small bowl. Rub this mixture evenly all over the steak. Allow it to stand for about 10 minutes at room temperature.

3. Take another bowl and add mango, cucumber, cilantro, lime juice, ginger, and salt to taste in it. Mix well. Cover it and let it chill.

4. With a cooking spray, spray adequate amount of it on both sides of the steak. Put it on a grill rack. Allow it to grill for about 5 minutes on each side until thoroughly cooked. Remove it from the grill and allow it to stand for about 5 minutes. Cut the steak into thin slices diagonally.

5. Serve it with the mango salsa.

HEALTHY CHIPOTLE POTATO SKINS

SERVING SIZE: 2
SERVINGS PER RECIPE: 16
CALORIES: 85
COOKING TIME: 1 HOUR 15 MINUTES

INGREDIENTS:

Baking potatoes—4, large, rinsed, dried
Extra-virgin olive oil—¼ cup, divided
Chipotle seasoning—1 teaspoon
Sea salt—½ teaspoon
Black pepper—½ teaspoon
Tomatoes—2, finely chopped
Sweet onion—1, finely chopped
Balsamic vinegar—2 tablespoons
Greek yogurt—½ cup, low fat

NUTRITION INFORMATION:

Carbohydrate—13 g
Protein—2 g
Fat—3 g
Sodium—78 mg
Cholesterol—7 mg

INSTRUCTIONS:

1. Preheat the oven to a temperature of 400°F.

2. Rub the potatoes with extra-virgin olive oil and wrap it in the foil. Put it on the baking sheet. Allow it to bake for an hour. Pierce it gently with a fork to check its tenderness.

3. Take a small bowl and add chipotle seasoning, remaining oil, salt, and pepper in it. Mix it well.

4. Once the potatoes are well cooked, cut them into quarters, and scoop out ½ of the inside pulp from every quarter. Discard the pulp.

5. While there is some pulp left inside it, add the oil and chipotle mixture into it. Allow it to bake for another 15 minutes.

6. Take another bowl and add onion, tomatoes, and balsamic vinegar in it. Combine it well.

7. Put one dollop of the Greek yogurt on top of the potato skins. Then add the tomato mixture at the top of it.

8. Your dish is ready to be served.

PARMESAN MUSHROOM CHICKEN

SERVING SIZE: 1
SERVINGS PER RECIPE: 4
CALORIES: 328
COOKING TIME: 30 MINUTES

INGREDIENTS:

Chicken breasts—4, halved, cut into strips
Garlic cloves—2, minced
Fresh parsley—1 tablespoon, minced
Olive oil—2 tablespoons
Mushrooms—8 ounces, drained, sliced
Half-and-half—½ cup
Parmesan—1/3 cup
Salt—to taste
Pepper—to taste

NUTRITION INFORMATION:

Carbohydrate—28 g
Protein –89 g
Fat—22 g
Sodium—2366 mg
Cholesterol—41 mg

INSTRUCTIONS:

1. Preheat the oven at a temperature of 350°F.

2. Spray the 11 × 7 inch baking dish with a cooking spray.

3. Take a sauté pan and add olive oil in it. Allow it to heat. Sprinkle salt and pepper on top of the chicken. Let the chicken cook for about 2 minutes on each side. Put garlic, parsley, and mushrooms and sauté it for about few minutes.

4. Also, add cream and parmesan cheese and cook for few more minutes. Turn the heat off.

5. Transfer the entire thing to the baking dish. Sprinkle some more parmesan on top of it. Allow it to bake for about 25 minutes.

6. Your dish is ready to be served.

CITRUS AND HERB CRUSTED SALMON

SERVING SIZE: 1
SERVINGS PER RECIPE: 2
CALORIES: 612
COOKING TIME: 20 MINUTES

INGREDIENTS:

- Brown sugar—1 teaspoon
- Lemon zest—1 teaspoon
- Orange zest—1 teaspoon
- Parsley—2 tablespoons, finely chopped
- Coriander—1 teaspoon, ground
- Fresh thyme—1 teaspoon, finely chopped
- Black pepper—½ teaspoon, freshly ground
- Kosher salt—1 teaspoon
- Olive oil—3 tablespoons
- Salmon fillets—1 pound

NUTRITION INFORMATION:

- Carbohydrate–25 g
- Protein—85 g
- Fat—34 g
- Sodium—856 mg
- Cholesterol—23 mg

INSTRUCTIONS:

1. Preheat the oven to a temperature of 450°F.

2. Take a small bowl and add lemon zest, brown sugar, orange zest, parsley, thyme, coriander, salt, pepper, and olive oil in it. Combine it well.

3. Put the rubbed salmon on a baking sheet. Pat it dry. Rub the citrus and herb mixture into the fish and spread it evenly.

4. Allow it to bake for about 15 minutes until the fish is well cooked and flaky. Remove it from the oven.

5. Your dish is ready to be served.

THAI PORK SPRING ROLLS

SERVING SIZE: 2
SERVINGS PER RECIPE: 10
CALORIES: 462
COOKING TIME: 10 MINUTES

INGREDIENTS:

Vermicelli noodles—50 g
Sesame oil—1 tablespoon
Pork—200 g, minced
Garlic clove—1, crushed
Red chili—1, finely diced
Coriander roots—2, finely diced
Fish sauce—1 teaspoon
Sugar—1 teaspoon
Coriander leaves—2 tablespoons, diced
Spring rolls—1 packet
Cold water—2 tablespoons

NUTRITION INFORMATION:

Carbohydrate—35 g
Protein—23 g
Fat—12 g
Sodium—336 mg
Cholesterol—16 mg

INSTRUCTIONS:

1. Prepare hot water and put the noodles in it. Let the noodles soak in the hot water and turn soft. Drain the noodles and cut it into small lengths.

2. Take a wok and add oil in it. Let the oil heat well. Add the garlic, chili, pork mince, and coriander root in it. Cook until the pork is thoroughly cooked through. Now add the sugar, fish sauce, and coriander leaves in it. Allow it to cook until the pork is fully cooked.

3. Remove it from the heat. Stir well. Allow it to stand until the juices are well absorbed.

4. Place a spring roll sheet on the plate. Put some filling diagonally across it. First, fold the top part of it and then fold the sides. On the other end, brush some water on it to seal it well. Roll the sheet and deep-fry it until golden in color.

5. Your dish is ready to be served.

AVOCADO STUFFED CHICKEN BREASTS

SERVING SIZE: 2
SERVINGS PER RECIPE: 2
CALORIES: 196
COOKING TIME: 22 MINUTES

INGREDIENTS:

Chicken breasts—4, large
All-purpose seasoning blend
Avocado—1, large, diced
Sun-dried tomato—¼ cup, strips dipped in oil, drained and diced
Cilantro—2 tablespoons, chopped
Salt—¼ teaspoon
Extra-virgin olive oil—2 tablespoons

NUTRITION INFORMATION:

Carbohydrate—57 g
Protein—45 g
Fat—10 g
Sodium—360 mg
Cholesterol—21 mg

INSTRUCTIONS:

1. Preheat the oven at a temperature of 425°F.

2. Take the chicken breasts and make a pocket on it by slicing it with a knife. Repeat on each side.

3. Season the chicken breasts with the seasoning blends on each side.

4. Take a small bowl and add sun-dried tomatoes, diced avocado, cilantro, and salt in it. Mix it well. Divide the mixture evenly between the chicken breasts. Close the pockets with the help of a toothpick.

5. In a skillet, add oil over medium heat. Put olive oil in it and once hot, sear the chicken into it for about 3 minutes on both the sides. Make sure it is seared until golden brown in color.

6. Cover the pan with the aluminum foil and put it inside the preheated oven for about 15 minutes. The chicken should reach an internal temperature of 155°F.

7. Remove it from the oven and serve.

GRILLED PINEAPPLE BARBEQUE CHICKEN

SERVING SIZE: 6 OUNCES CHICKEN AND 2 PINEAPPLE SLICES
SERVINGS PER RECIPE: 4
CALORIES: 270
COOKING TIME: 15 MINUTES

INGREDIENTS:

Chicken breast—1.33 pounds, boneless and skinless
Barbeque sauce—½ cup
Pineapple juice—¼ cup
Soy sauce—2 tablespoons
Garlic clove—1, minced
Ginger—1 teaspoon, minced
Sriracha—1 teaspoon
Pineapple—2 cups, sliced

NUTRITION INFORMATION:

Carbohydrate—25 g
Protein—33 g
Fat—2 g
Sodium—790 mg
Cholesterol—74 mg

INSTRUCTIONS:

1. Take a small bowl and add pineapple juice, barbeque sauce, soy sauce, ginger, garlic, and Sriracha in it. Mix it well. Marinade the chicken with this mixture for about 30 minutes. It would be best if the marinade is kept overnight.

2. Remove the chicken from the marinade and let it drip off the excess marinade.

3. With the help of a cooking spray, make sure the pineapple slices are sprayed well.

4. Allow the chicken and the pineapple slices to grill for about 5 minutes on each side. Make sure everything is thoroughly cooked through. If the chicken is not thick enough, allow it to cook for less time on each side.

5. Take a saucepan and pour the marinade mixture in it. Bring it to a boil. Allow it to cook for about 4–5 minutes until it has slightly reduced. Drizzle it on the chicken and also the pineapple slices.

6. Your dish is ready to be served.

BACON CHEESEBURGER SKILLET

SERVING SIZE: 1
SERVINGS PER RECIPE: 4
CALORIES: 435
COOKING TIME: 30 MINUTES

INGREDIENTS:

Lean ground beef—1 pound
Turkey bacon—4 slices, coarsely chopped
Dijon mustard—2 teaspoons
Worcestershire sauce—2 teaspoons
Garlic powder—1 teaspoon
Red onion—½ cup, finely diced
Tomatoes—1 can, 14 ounces, drained
Cheddar cheese—¾ cup, shredded
Salt—to taste
Black pepper—to taste

NUTRITION INFORMATION:

Carbohydrate—24 g
Protein—76 g
Fat—52 g
Sodium—4567 mg
Cholesterol—125 mg

INSTRUCTIONS:

1. Take a large skillet and add the turkey bacon in it. Cook until thoroughly cooked to your liking. Remove it from the skillet. Dice it into small pieces.

2. Add the beef in the skillet and let it brown by breaking it while it cooks.

3. Once the beef has turned brown in color, put all the ingredients in it and combine it well.

4. Cover it and allow it to simmer on low heat for about 10–15 minutes. Stir it occasionally.

5. Sprinkle the cheese all over the meat until melted.

6. You can serve it over the fresh lettuce.

7. Your dish is ready to be served.

CUCUMBER TUNA SALAD BITES

SERVING SIZE: 1
SERVINGS PER RECIPE: 4
CALORIES: 159
COOKING TIME: 15 MINUTES

INGREDIENTS:

Chunk light tuna in water—1 can, 5 ounces, drained well
Red onion soaked in cold water—2 teaspoons, drained and rinsed
Celery—1 tablespoon, minced
Dill—1 tablespoon, minced
Mayo—¼ cup
Fresh lemon juice—½ teaspoon
Black pepper—1/8 teaspoon
Cucumbers—2
Grape tomatoes—3, sliced into quarters
Dill sprigs—for garnishing

NUTRITION INFORMATION:

Carbohydrate—7 g
Protein—8 g
Fat—12 g
Sodium—178 mg
Cholesterol—18 mg

INSTRUCTIONS:

1. Take a bowl and add red onion, tuna, celery, mayo, dill, lemon juice, and black pepper in it. Mix it well with the help of a fork. Make sure it is evenly combined.

2. Peel off the cucumbers and cut it into half-inch slices. Scoop out the center of the cucumber using a melon baller. Make near about 12 cucumber cups like these.

3. Scoop a spoonful of the tuna salad inside the cucumber slice.

4. Garnish it with grape tomatoes and a small sprig of the dill.

5. Your dish is ready to be served.

BAKED SCALLOPS

SERVING SIZE: 1
SERVINGS PER RECIPE: 4
CALORIES: 363
COOKING TIME: 20 MINUTES

INGREDIENTS:

Butter—4 tablespoons, melted
Bay scallops—1 ½ pounds, rinsed, drained
Seasoned dry bread crumbs—½ cup
Onion powder—1 teaspoon
Garlic powder—1 teaspoon
Paprika—½ teaspoon
Dried parsley—½ teaspoon
Garlic cloves—3, minced
Parmesan cheese—¼ cup, grated

NUTRITION INFORMATION:

Carbohydrate—16 g
Protein—31 g
Fat—19 g
Sodium—565 mg
Cholesterol—88 mg

INSTRUCTIONS:

1. Preheat the oven at a temperature of 400°F.

2. Take a casserole dish and pour the melted butter into it. Put the scallops in it. Spread the butter and scallops evenly across the dish.

3. Take a small bowl and add bread crumbs in it along with garlic powder, onion powder, minced garlic, parsley, paprika, and parmesan cheese. Mix well. Now spread this mixture all over the scallops.

4. Let it bake in preheated oven until firm. Cook for about 20 minutes.

5. Your dish is ready to be served.

BUTTER CHICKEN

SERVING SIZE: 1
SERVINGS PER RECIPE: 8
CALORIES: 346
COOKING TIME: 50 MINUTES

INGREDIENTS:

Raw chicken—700 g

FOR THE MARINADE:

Red chili powder—1 teaspoon
Ginger and garlic paste—1 teaspoon
Salt—to taste
Curd—½ kg

FOR THE GRAVY:

White butter—175 g
Black cumin seeds—½ teaspoon
Tomato puree—½ kg
Sugar—1 1/2 teaspoons
Red chili powder—1 teaspoon
Salt—to taste
Fresh cream—100 g
Green chilies—4, sliced
Fenugreek leaves—½ teaspoon, crushed

NUTRITION INFORMATION:

Carbohydrate—5 g
Protein—22 g
Fat—26 g
Sodium—582 mg
Cholesterol—116 mg

INSTRUCTIONS:

1. Take a mixing bowl and add red chili powder, salt, ginger garlic paste, and curd in it. Mix it well.

2. Now add the chicken pieces in the marinade and mix again. Put it inside the refrigerator for about 6 hours or overnight.

3. You can roast the chicken in the tandoor or oven as per your choice. Let it roast for 10–12 minutes until it is almost done.

4. To prepare the chicken gravy, add half of the white butter in the pan. Allow it to heat up. Add the tomato puree in the pan and sauté for about 3 minutes. Put sugar, cumin seeds, salt, and red chili powder in it. Combine it well.

5. Put the prepared chicken, white butter, sliced green chilies, fresh cream, and crushed fenugreek leaves in it. Sauté it for about 3 minutes. Allow the chicken to cook until done.

6. Your dish is ready to be served.

BLACK FOREST CRUMBLE

SERVING SIZE: 1
SERVINGS PER RECIPE: 6
CALORIES: 173
COOKING TIME: 40 MINUTES

INGREDIENTS:

FOR THE FRUIT:

    Black forest frozen fruit—500 g
    Maple syrup—¼ cup
    Vanilla extract—1 teaspoon
    Cherry brandy—2 tablespoons, optional

FOR THE CRUMBLE:

    75% Dark chocolate—100 g
    Oats—2 cups, coarsely ground
    Maple syrup—2 tablespoons
    Vanilla extract—½ teaspoon

TO SERVE:

    Vegan ice cream

NUTRITION INFORMATION:

Carbohydrate—40 g
Protein—6 g
Fat—2 g
Sodium—28 mg
Cholesterol—0 mg

INSTRUCTIONS:

1. Preheat the oven to a temperature of 180°C.

2. Grease the baking dish well. Put fruit, vanilla extract, maple syrup, and cherry brandy in a bowl. Mix it well and pour it on the baking dish. Spread it out.

3. In a double boiler, melt the chocolate along with vanilla and maple syrup. Take a food processor and coarsely grind the oats well in it. Once the chocolate has melted, add the oats in it. Combine it well. Spread this mixture evenly over the fruit base. Allow it to bake it for 30 minutes approximately.

4. Serve it with vegan ice cream.

CHEESESTEAK STUFFED PEPPERS

SERVING SIZE: 1
SERVINGS PER RECIPE: 4
CALORIES: 311
COOKING TIME: 30 MINUTES

INGREDIENTS:

Roast beef—8 ounces, thinly sliced
Provolone cheese—8 slices
Green bell peppers—2, large
Sweet onion—1, medium
Baby bella mushrooms—1 package, 6 ounces
Butter—2 tablespoons
Olive oil—2 tablespoons
Garlic—1 tablespoon, minced

NUTRITION INFORMATION:

Carbohydrate—56 g
Protein—43 g
Fat—18 g
Sodium—2466 mg
Cholesterol—543 mg

INSTRUCTIONS:

1. Take the peppers and slice it into halves lengthwise. Remove the ribs and the seeds.

2. Now slice the onions and the mushrooms. Take a pan and put butter and olive oil in it. Add the sliced onions and mushrooms along with salt and pepper for seasoning. Allow it to sauté over medium heat. Sauté it until the onions and mushrooms are well caramelized for about 25 minutes.

3. Preheat the oven at a temperature of 400°C.

4. Take the roasted beef and slice it into thin strips. Put this in the onion and mushroom mixture. Let it cook for about 10 minutes.

5. Line the peppers with a slice of provolone cheese.

6. Now put the meat mixture into these peppers.

7. Put another slice of the provolone cheese on each pepper.

8. Allow it to bake it for 20 minutes. Let the cheese on the top turn golden brown in color.

9. Your dish is ready to be served.

CHICKEN PALERMO

SERVING SIZE: 1
SERVINGS PER RECIPE: 4
CALORIES: 834
COOKING TIME: 20 MINUTES

INGREDIENTS:

Chicken cutlets—4, 6 ounces each, boneless and skinless
Flour—½ cup
Unsalted butter—4 ounces
Garlic—1 tablespoon, chopped
Dry white wine—1 cup
Chicken stock—1 cup
Prosciutto—4 ounces, thinly sliced
Provolone—4 ounces, sharply sliced
Roasted red peppers—4 ounces, sliced
Roasted yellow peppers—4 ounces, sliced
Unsalted butter—4 ounces, cut into 1-inch pieces

NUTRITION INFORMATION:

Carbohydrate—10 g
Protein—57 g
Fat—59 g
Sodium—1525 mg
Cholesterol—262 mg

INSTRUCTIONS:

1. Put the chicken in a dish and coat it well with flour on all the sides. Get rid of the excess flour by shaking it once coated.

2. Take a large skillet and put the butter in it over medium-high heat. Put the chicken in it and cook until the bottom of the chicken turns golden brown for about 2 minutes.

3. Turn the chicken over and put the garlic in it. Sauté the garlic until it turns brown in color for about 1–2 minutes.

4. Now add the chicken stock and the wine. Reduce the heat of the skillet and allow it to simmer for about 8 minutes uncovered.

5. Take each chicken cutlet and top it with prosciutto, roasted peppers, and provolone. Sprinkle salt and pepper as desired. Allow it to simmer for another 5 minutes. Add the butter cubes, one at a time to thicken the sauce.

6. Transfer the chicken to the plates. Add sauce on top of each chicken.

7. Your dish is ready to be served.

GREEK-STYLE LEMON CHICKEN SKEWERS

SERVING SIZE: 1
SERVINGS PER RECIPE: 4
CALORIES: 245
COOKING TIME: 15 MINUTES
INGREDIENTS:

Lemon juice—¼ cup
Olive oil—1/4 cup
Fresh rosemary—1 sprig, finely minced
Garlic cloves—3, finely minced
Oregano—1 teaspoon
Chili flakes—1 teaspoon
Chicken breast—2 pounds, skinless, cut into medium pieces
Whole milk Greek yogurt—1 ½ cups
Fresh mint—1/3 cup, finely minced
Garlic clove—1, small, finely minced
Olive oil—1 tablespoon
Kosher salt—to taste
Black pepper—to taste
Lemon wedges—as required

NUTRITION INFORMATION:

Carbohydrate—52 g
Protein—3 g
Fat—7 g
Sodium—34 mg
Cholesterol—12 mg

INSTRUCTIONS:

1. Take a medium bowl and add olive oil, lemon juice, three garlic cloves, chili flakes, oregano, and rosemary in it. Put the chicken in it and stir it well. Put it inside the refrigerator for an hour at least. It would be best if refrigerated for about 4 hours.

2. Take another small bowl and add 1 garlic clove, mint, yogurt, and olive oil in it. Mix well. Sprinkle salt and pepper as desired. Now cover the bowl and put it inside the refrigerator.

3. Make the bamboo skewers ready by soaking it in the water for about 30 minutes.

4. Preheat the griller at a temperature of 425°C. Remove the chicken and also the yogurt sauce 30 minutes beforehand from the refrigerator.

5. Now thread the chicken in the skewers.

6. Put it on the hot grill and cook until the chicken is well cooked and loosens itself from the grill. Let it cook for about 5 minutes and turn the skewers over. Keep grilling the chicken until the temperature of the thickest part of the meat reaches 160°C.

7. Remove the chicken from the grill and take it out from the skewers. Place the chicken on the serving dish.

8. To caramelize the lemon wedges, put it on the hot grill for about sometime.

9. Plate the grilled chicken with seasoned yogurt. Also, serve the grilled lemons on the side. Your dish is ready to be served.

PERSIAN BEEF KEBABS

SERVING SIZE: 2
SERVINGS PER RECIPE: 4
CALORIES: 212
COOKING TIME: 10 MINUTES
INGREDIENTS:

Sirloin steak—2 pounds
White onion—1, medium, roughly chopped
Garlic cloves—5, medium, crushed
Lime—1, medium, juiced, 4 teaspoons
Kosher salt—2 tablespoons
Freshly ground black pepper—2 teaspoons
Saffron—2 pinches, steeped in 2 tablespoons of boiling water
Roma tomatoes—8, medium
Olive oil—as required

FOR SERVING

Bread
Plain yogurt
Cilantro leaves

NUTRITION INFORMATION:

Carbohydrate—24g
Protein—33 g
Fat—46 g
Sodium—38 mg
Cholesterol—40 mg

INSTRUCTIONS:

1. Trim all the excess fats from the steak. Cut the steak into 1-inch cubes. Put it in a bowl.

2. In a food processor, add lime juice, onion, garlic, salt, and pepper along with the saffron. Process it well until smooth. Now pour this mixture all over the meat and coat it well. Cover it and allow it to marinade for about 30 minutes at normal room temperature. You can also keep it inside the refrigerator for about 12 hours.

3. Keep the griller ready by setting the heat to 350°F or medium heat. Oil it well with the help of a brush.

4. Make the bamboo skewers ready by soaking it in the water for about 30 minutes.

5. Thread the meat in the skewers and make sure there is some space left in between the threaded meat.

6. Take a small bowl and add tomatoes in it. Drizzle oil all over it. Sprinkle salt and pepper as desired and toss it well to coat it thoroughly. Put the meat and the tomatoes on the grill. Allow it to cook well and turn once until medium rare. Let it grill for about 7–10 minutes. Keep cooking the tomatoes and turning it rarely until soft for about 10 minutes.

7. Remove the meat from the skewers and place it on a plate. The kebabs are ready.

8. To make sandwiches, assemble the beef kebabs, tomatoes, yogurt, and cilantro inside the breads.

9. Your dish is ready to be served.

LOBSTER SALAD COCKTAIL

SERVING SIZE: 1
SERVINGS PER RECIPE: 4
CALORIES: 195
COOKING TIME: 10 MINUTES

INGREDIENTS:

Mayonnaise—1/3 cup

Lemon zest—1 teaspoon

Lemon—1, juiced

Salt—to taste

Freshly ground black pepper—to taste

Celery—1 stalk, finely chopped

Shallot—1, finely chopped

Fresh tarragon leaves—1 tablespoon, finely chopped

Chives—1 tablespoon, finely chopped

Lobster tails—3, 1 pound, chopped

Lemon slices—for garnishing

Dry rub—for garnishing

NUTRITION INFORMATION:

Carbohydrate—23 g

Protein—16 g

Fat—13 g

Sodium—287 mg

Cholesterol—94 mg

INSTRUCTIONS:

1. In a small bowl, add mayonnaise, lemon juice, lemon zest, celery, salt, pepper, shallot, chives, and tarragon in it. Mix it well.

2. Now add the lobster meat to the mayonnaise sauce and mix it.

3. Take four martini glasses and rub the rim of it with a lemon.

4. Put the glasses in the dry rub.

5. Evenly divide the lobster salad into four glasses.

6. Garnish it with lemon slices and dry rub.

7. Your dish is ready to be served.

CAJUN OMELET

SERVING SIZE: 1
SERVINGS PER RECIPE: 4
CALORIES: 103
COOKING TIME: 22 MINUTES

INGREDIENTS:

- Butter—5 teaspoons, divided
- Andouille sausage—1 ¼ cups, sliced
- Plum tomatoes—2, small, seeded, chopped
- Onion—1/2, medium, chopped
- Red bell pepper—½, medium, chopped
- Celery rib—1, chopped
- Garlic—1 teaspoon, minced
- Creole seasoning—1 teaspoon, divided
- Eggs—12, large
- Fresh parsley—1 tablespoon, chopped
- Vegetable cooking spray—as required
- Monterey jack cheese—1 ½ cups, 6 ounces, shredded
- Hot sauce—as required

NUTRITION INFORMATION:

Carbohydrate—4 g
Protein—3 g
Fat—1 g
Sodium—356 mg
Cholesterol—55 mg

INSTRUCTIONS:

1. Take a heavy skillet and put 1 teaspoon of butter in it. Melt it over medium-high heat. Now add the sausage and cook for about 6 minutes by stirring occasionally. Make sure the sausage is well browned. Put tomatoes and the next four ingredients along with ½ teaspoon of the Creole seasoning. Allow it to cook for about 5 minutes until the vegetables turn tender. Remove it from the skillet.

2. Take a small bowl and add eggs, remaining Creole seasoning, and parsley in it. Whisk it well.

3. In another skillet, spray the inside with cooking spray. Put 1 teaspoon of the butter in the skillet on medium heat. Make sure the skillet is evenly coated with the butter. Pour about 1/4th of the egg mixture in it. Once the eggs start to cook, lift the edges to help the uncooked liquid to flow underneath the cooked portion. Cover it and let it cook for a minute.

4. Put 1/4th of the sausage mixture along with the cheese on half side of the omelet. Fold the omelet over the filling.

5. The omelet is ready to be served. Repeat the same procedure in three batches.

6. Serve it with hot sauce!

TANGY SESAME LEMON CHICKEN
SERVING SIZE: 1
SERVINGS PER RECIPE: 4
CALORIES: 599
COOKING TIME: 15 MINUTES

INGREDIENTS:

FOR THE SESAME LEMON SAUCE:

Lemon zest—2
Lemon juiced—2
Honey—2 tablespoons
Sesame oil—1 teaspoon
Turmeric—¼ teaspoon
Cornstarch—2 teaspoons

FOR THE CHICKEN:

Chicken thighs—8, boneless and skinless
Cornstarch—3 tablespoons
Coconut oil—2 tablespoons
Ginger—1 teaspoon, minced
Garlic clove—1, minced
Bok choy—10 ounces
Cauliflower rice—for serving
Sesame seeds—for garnishing
Lemon slices—for garnishing

NUTRITION INFORMATION:

Carbohydrate—16 g
Protein—77 g
Fat—24 g
Sodium—375 mg
Cholesterol—362 mg

INSTRUCTIONS:

1. Take a medium bowl and add lemon zest, lemon juice, sesame oil, honey, and turmeric in it. In another bowl, whisk the cornstarch with some water. Add this mixture in the other bowl. Stir well.

2. Get rid of all the excess fat from the chicken thighs and cut it into 5–6 pieces. Put it inside the plastic bag and sprinkle some cornstarch in it. Shake the bag well so that the chicken is well coated with the cornstarch.

3. Take a large frying pan and add coconut oil in it. Put it on medium-high heat. Now add the chicken and allow it to cook until brown from all the sides. Make sure the chicken is thoroughly cooked through for about 10 minutes. Remove the chicken and transfer it to a plate.

4. Add garlic and ginger in the pan and cook for some time. Put the bok choy in it and cook until the leaves start wilting for about 2 minutes. Remove it from the pan.

5. Put the chicken back in the pan and pour the prepared sauce all over it. Stir well for about a minute until the sauce thickens.

6. The sesame lemon chicken is ready.

7. Serve it with cauliflower rice. Garnish it with sesame seeds on the top and lemon slices on the sides.

8. Your dish is ready to be served.

ONE POT CHICKEN AND MUSHROOM RISOTTO

SERVING SIZE: 1
SERVINGS PER RECIPE: 4
CALORIES: 615
COOKING TIME: 35 MINUTES

INGREDIENTS:

Butter—60 g
Onion—1, large, finely chopped
Thyme sprigs—2, leaves picked
Chestnut mushrooms—250-g pack, sliced
Risotto rice—300 g
Cooked chicken—200 g, chopped into chunks
Parmesan—50 g, grated
Parsley, finely chopped—as required

NUTRITION INFORMATION:

Carbohydrate—67 g
Protein—37 g
Fat—21 g
Sodium—0 mg
Cholesterol—0 mg

INSTRUCTIONS:

1. Take a large pan and heat the butter in it. Add the onion and cook for about 10 minutes until it turns soft. Add the thyme leaves and mushrooms. Stir well. Allow it to cook for about 5 minutes. Sprinkle the rice in it and stir it well to coat it with the mixture.

2. Pour a quarter portion of the stock and let it cook while stirring occasionally. Top it with more stock if required.

3. When the rice has absorbed most of the stock, add the chicken in it and stir again. Season it well. Stir the parsley and parmesan cheese in it. Sprinkle parmesan on the top if you prefer.

4. Your dish is ready to be served.

MUSSELS IN WHITE WINE AND GARLIC

SERVING SIZE: 1
SERVINGS PER RECIPE: 4
CALORIES: 366
COOKING TIME: 15 MINUTES

INGREDIENTS:

Mussels—4 pounds
Dry white wine—2 cups
Shallots—4, large, finely chopped
Garlic cloves—4, finely chopped
Salt—½ teaspoon
Mixed fresh herbs—1/3 cup
Butter—6 tablespoons, cut into pieces

NUTRITION INFORMATION:

Carbohydrate—47g
Protein—34 g
Fat—20 g
Sodium—3445 mg
Cholesterol—93 mg

INSTRUCTIONS:

1. Rinse the mussels well under the cold water.

2. Discard the strings from the mussels' shells, if any. You can use a knife for this step.

3. Take a large stockpot and set it on medium heat. Add garlic, shallots, white wine, and salt in it.

4. Allow it to simmer for about 5 minutes.

5. Add the mussels in it and cover it. Increase the heat to high heat.

6. Allow it to cook until the mussels open up, nearly about 5 minutes.

7. Add the herbs and the butter in it. Stir well.

8. Remove it from the heat.

9. Divide the cooked mussels and the broth in bowls.

10. Your dish is ready to be served.

TROPICAL FRUIT, AVOCADO, AND GRILLED SHRIMP SALAD

SERVING SIZE: 2
SERVINGS PER RECIPE: 6
CALORIES: 155
COOKING TIME: 20 MINUTES

INGREDIENTS:

Red onion—1, thinly sliced
Coarse salt—2 teaspoons
Pineapple—1, diced
Ripe papayas—2, diced
Ripe mango—1, diced
Roasted red bell pepper—1, cut into strips
Roasted yellow bell peppers—1, cut into strips
Poblano chilies—2, cut into ¼ inch strips
Jalapeno peppers—2, minced
Fresh cilantro—¼ cup, chopped
Extra-virgin olive oil—2/3 cup
Wine vinegar—1/3 cup
Shrimp—30, large, peeled, deveined
Ripe avocados—2, cut into wedges
Freshly ground black pepper—to taste

NUTRITION INFORMATION:

Carbohydrate—20 g
Protein—43 g
Fat—1 g
Sodium—0 mg
Cholesterol—0 mg

INSTRUCTIONS:

1. Sprinkle coarse salt on the onion slices in between your hands. Put the onions in a colander for about 15 minutes. Take out all the liquid from it by squeezing it into batches.

2. Take a large bowl and add onions, pineapple, and also the next seven ingredients together in it. Add olive oil and vinegar in it. Mix it well. Toss it along with the fruit mixture.

3. Grill the shrimps in a griller for about 3 minutes until opaque on both the sides. Toss it in the salad. Stir in the avocado. Sprinkle salt and black pepper as desired.

4. Your dish is ready to be served.

BOK CHOY WITH GARLIC, HONEY AND SOY
SERVING SIZE: 1
SERVINGS PER RECIPE: 4
CALORIES: 381
COOKING TIME: 5 MINUTES
INGREDIENTS:

Peanut oil—1 tablespoon
Bok choy—2 bunches, washed, quartered
Garlic cloves—2, thinly sliced
Honey—1 tablespoon
Soy sauce—2 tablespoons
Sesame oil—¼ teaspoon

NUTRITION INFORMATION:

Carbohydrate—8 g
Protein—3 g
Fat—5 g
Sodium—660 mg
Cholesterol—0 mg

INSTRUCTIONS:

1. Take a large wok and heat oil in it over high heat. Coat the entire wok with the oil.

2. Put the bok Choy in it. Stir-fry it for about 2 minutes.

3. Make sure it is wilted. Now add the garlic, soy sauce, and honey in it.

4. Stir-fry again for another 3 minutes. Make sure the bok Choy turns tender.

5. Toss it again in the sesame oil.

6. Serve it with grilled chicken!

ROASTED RED PEPPER QUINOA

SERVING SIZE: 1
SERVINGS PER RECIPE: 4
CALORIES: 231
COOKING TIME: 20 MINUTES

INGREDIENTS:

Onion—1, diced
Garlic cloves—4, minced
Olive oil—2 tablespoons
Quinoa—2 cups
Water—3 ½ cups
Juice from roasted red peppers—½ cup
Salt—1 tablespoon
Roasted red peppers—½ cup, chopped

NUTRITION INFORMATION:

Carbohydrate—7 g
Protein—4 g
Fat—2 g
Sodium—490 mg
Cholesterol—170 mg

INSTRUCTIONS:

1. To make it in a rice maker, first of all, take a skillet. Put some olive oil in it and add the onions in it. Sauté it until translucent. Now add the garlic in it and sauté it again.

2. Add onions, garlic, and if the remaining oil inside the rice maker.

3. Add the red pepper juice, water, quinoa, and salt in it. Cover it well and start the cooking process in the rice maker. Once the rice maker makes the sound once done cooking, add the roasted red peppers in it.

4. Make sure you stir in between to avoid sticking of the ingredients.

5. Your dish is ready to be served.

CREAMY TUSCAN GARLIC CHICKEN

SERVING SIZE: 1
SERVINGS PER RECIPE: 6
CALORIES: 172
COOKING TIME: 15 MINUTES

INGREDIENTS:

Chicken breasts—1 ½ pounds, boneless, skinless and thinly sliced
Olive oil—2 tablespoons
Heavy cream—1 cup
Chicken broth—½ cup
Garlic powder—1 teaspoon
Italian seasoning—1 teaspoon
Parmesan cheese—½ cup
Spinach—1 cup, chopped
Sun-dried tomatoes—½ cup

NUTRITION INFORMATION:

Carbohydrate—38 g
Protein—12 g
Fat—2 g
Sodium—54 mg
Cholesterol—28 mg

INSTRUCTIONS:

1. Take a large skillet and put olive oil in it. Add the chicken in it and allow it to cook on medium-high heat for about 5 minutes on each side. Make sure the chicken is slightly brown in color and no longer pink. Remove the chicken from the skillet. Set it aside.

2. Now add the chicken broth, heavy cream, Italian seasoning, and garlic powder and parmesan cheese in it. Whisk it well over medium-high heat. Make sure it thickens well. Now add the spinach and also the sundried tomatoes and allow it to simmer until the spinach begins to wilt. Put the chicken back in the pan.

3. Your dish is ready to be served.

MISSISSIPPI SPICED CHICKEN WRAPS

SERVING SIZE: 1
SERVINGS PER RECIPE: 2
CALORIES: 870
COOKING TIME: 30 MINUTES

INGREDIENTS:

Sweet potato wedges—450 g
Lime—1
Onion marmalade—1 tablespoon
Baby spinach—1 bag
Chicken mini fillets—280 g
Mississippi-style spice mix—1 ½ teaspoons
Crème fraîche—1 pot
Fresh chili jam—1 tablespoon
Wholemeal tortilla—4

NUTRITION INFORMATION:

Carbohydrate—103 g
Protein—62 g
Fat—25 g
Sodium—0 mg
Cholesterol—0 mg

INSTRUCTIONS:

1. Take a baking tray and put the sweet potatoes in it.

2. Drizzle some oil all over the sweet potatoes. Sprinkle salt and pepper as desired. Toss it well.

3. Put it on the oven and allow it to roast it until soft and golden in color. Let it roast for about 15 minutes. Turn it over halfway through.

4. Take a bowl and add the chicken mini fillets in it. Drizzle some more oil in it. Sprinkle salt and pepper as required for the Mississippi spice mix. Coat the chicken well with the spices.

5. Take a frying pan and heat it over medium-high heat. Do not add any oil here. Add the chicken pieces and let it brown on each side for about 5 minutes. Make sure the chicken is thoroughly cooked and no longer pink in the middle.

6. In another bowl, add the lime zest along with the crème fraîche.

7. While in the other bowl, add the onion marmalade with the chili jam. Mix it well. Cut the lime into halves.

8. Once the chicken is done cooking, remove it from the heat. Squeeze lime juice on top of it and add the baby spinach into the pan. Toss it well to combine. Make sure the spinach soften well.

9. Plate the wrap and smear it with the onion-chili jam. Put the chicken on top of it. Place the spinach in the middle of it. Drizzle the prepared lime crème fraîche and roll up the wraps.

10. Your dish is ready to be served.

BOILED SALMON WITH MEDITERRANEAN COLESLAW

SERVING SIZE: 1
SERVINGS PER RECIPE: 4
CALORIES: 304
COOKING TIME: 15 MINUTES

INGREDIENTS:

Salmon—1 pound
Rosemary citrus seasoning—1 tablespoon
Extra-virgin olive oil—4 tablespoons
Unsalted butter—2 tablespoons
Coarse black pepper—1 teaspoon
Kosher salt—to taste
Roma tomatoes—2, large, sliced

FOR THE COLESLAW:
Cabbage—5 ounces, shredded
Bell peppers—¼ cup, sliced
Green onion stalks—3, medium, sliced
Italian parsley—1 tablespoon, chopped
Mint—1 tablespoon, chopped
All-purpose Greek seasoning—1 tablespoon
Extra-virgin olive oil—¼ cup
Feta cheese crumbles—3 ounces
White wine vinegar—2 tablespoons
Lemon juice—1
Coarse black pepper—1 tablespoon

NUTRITION INFORMATION:

Carbohydrate—4 g
Protein—8 g
Fat—1 g
Sodium—86 mg
Cholesterol—2 mg

INSTRUCTIONS:

1. Take a large mixing bowl and add all the coleslaw ingredients in it. Mix it well. Put it inside the refrigerator while preparing the salmon.

2. Clean the salmon properly and carefully remove the skin from it.

3. Preheat the oven.

4. Cut the salmon into four portions and add it in a mixing bowl. Add the rosemary citrus seasoning along with the olive oil. Season it with salt and pepper as desired. Brush the salmon fillets on both the sides. Put a small butter cube on top of every fillet.

5. Place it in the broiler for about 10 minutes. Make sure that you do not overcook the salmon.

6. Plate the grilled salmon along with the coleslaw. Drizzle some olive oil on top of it. You can add some extra butter on the top of the salmon. Add tomato slices on the sides. Season it with salt and pepper as desired.

7. Your dish is ready to be served.

SMOKY PORK AND BLACK BEAN TACOS1

SERVING SIZE: 1
SERVINGS PER RECIPE: 4
CALORIES: 592
COOKING TIME: 15 MINUTES

INGREDIENTS:

Vegetable oil—2 teaspoon
Red onion—1/2, chopped
Smoked paprika—2 teaspoon
Ground cumin—2 teaspoon
Lean pork mince—500 g
Passata—300 ml
Barbeque sauce—5 tablespoons
Black bean—400-g can, drained
Small bunch coriander, chopped—as required
Taco shells—8
Ripe avocado—1, peeled, sliced
Iceberg lettuce—½, finely shredded
Sour cream—for serving

NUTRITION INFORMATION:

Carbohydrate—45 g
Protein—38 g
Fat—29 g
Sodium—0 mg
Cholesterol—0 mg

INSTRUCTIONS:

1. Take a large frying pan and add oil in it. Heat the oil and put the onions in it. Allow it to cook for about 5 minutes until soft. Sprinkle it over the spices and allow it to cook for another minute. Put the mince in it. Break the mince with the help of a wooden spoon and stir it well.

2. Add the passata and barbeque sauce in the pan. Also, add 4 tablespoons of the water. Increase the heat and let the sauce bubble. Reduce the sauce to a thick consistency. Now add the beans and sprinkle salt and pepper as desired. Allow it to cook for about 2 minutes. Stir well. Add the coriander in it.

3. Heat the tacos according to the directions given in the package.

4. Plate the tacos and fill it with the pork and the bean mixture. Add avocado slices, shredded iceberg lettuce, and sour cream as desired.

5. Your dish is ready to be served.

LOW CARB CAULIFLOWER PIZZA CRUST

SERVING SIZE: 1
SERVINGS PER RECIPE: 4
CALORIES: 112
COOKING TIME: 20 MINUTES

INGREDIENTS:

Head of cauliflower—1, medium, yields 2 cups
Parmesan cheese—¼ cup
Mozzarella cheese—¼ cup
Egg—1
Salt—¼ teaspoon
Garlic powder—½ teaspoon
Basil—½ teaspoon, minced
Oregano—½ teaspoon, minced
Marinara sauce—1 cup
Mozzarella cheese—2 cups

NUTRITION INFORMATION:

Carbohydrate—7 g
Protein—8 g
Fat—6 g
Sodium—413 mg
Cholesterol—38 mg

INSTRUCTIONS:

1. Preheat the oven at a temperature of 500°F.

2. Cut the stems of the cauliflower and discard. Cut the cauliflower into chunks. In a food processor, add the cauliflower and pulse it well.

3. In a microwave safe bowl, add the processed cauliflower in it. Microwave it uncovered for about 5 minutes on high heat. Once done, remove it from the microwave. Let it cool for about 5 minutes. After the cauliflower has cooled down, put it in a clean kitchen towel and squeeze all the liquid out of it. Make sure all the liquid has been squeezed out.

4. Take a bowl and add the cauliflower in it. Add the garlic, egg, cheese, and the rest of the seasoning in it. Mix it well. Keep stirring until the texture is capable of dough.

5. On a pizza pan, spread the entire cauliflower mixture. This is for making the pizza crust. Let the crust bake for about 15 minutes. The crust should turn crispy and golden. Remove it from the oven. Add all the toppings such as the marinara sauce and cheese on it. You can also add extra toppings if you like.

6. Put the pizza in the oven and put the broiler on. Allow it to bake for about 5 minutes. Let the cheese melt.

7. Your dish is ready to be served.

CHICKEN KORMA CAULIFLOWER RICE

SERVING SIZE: 1
SERVINGS PER RECIPE: 2
CALORIES: 631
COOKING TIME: 20 MINUTES

INGREDIENTS:

Chicken breast fillet—150 g, skinless
Garlic cloves—4
Ground ginger—¼ teaspoon
Single cream light—60 ml
Red chili flakes—¼ teaspoon, crushed
Butter—1 tablespoon
Ground coriander—¼ teaspoon
Garam masala—¼ teaspoon
Ground black pepper—¼ teaspoon
Coconut cream—60 g
Ground almonds—10 g
Frozen cauliflower florets—120 g

NUTRITION INFORMATION:

Carbohydrate—13 g
Protein—60 g
Fat—39g
Sodium—0 mg
Cholesterol—0 mg

INSTRUCTIONS:

1. Take a large frying pan and add butter in it.

2. Cut the chicken into small pieces and put it in the frying pan. Fry it for around 10 minutes.

3. To defrost your cauliflower in the microwave, set the time to 5 minutes. Once the process is completed, set it aside. Let it cool down.

4. Take a small bowl and add all the spices and herbs in it. Mix it well.

5. In a pan, add sliced garlic and allow it to cook it for a few minutes.

6. Once the chicken is well cooked, put the coconut cream and the single cream in the pan.

7. Add the spice mix to it and stir well. Let it cook over medium heat for about 5 minutes. Also, add the ground almonds and stir well. Allow it to simmer for about 4 minutes.

8. Mix the cauliflower in the rice and plate it. Now add the chicken korma in the dish.

9. Your dish is ready to be served.

CONCLUSION

The Bright Line Eating movement is now practiced by over hundreds and thousands of people all over the world now. It is the solution everyone has been looking for to have a healthy life.

This long-term weight loss solution is effective and very well received by everyone who has ever opted for it. It talks of no shortcuts or miracles. It is simply the way one can change his/her lives to become happy, thin, and free. This revolutionizing treatment tries to work on the brain rather than the body.

It trains the brain, the master organ to function in a way that turns out to be most effective for weight loss. The Bright Line Eating is a psychological and neuroscientific weight loss strategy. Bright Line Eating helps in a paradigm shift of identity, which is necessary to stick with it long-term weight loss goals. It gives your life discipline, structure, and motivation to fight against all the extra pounds.

This Bright Line Eating Cookbook comes handy to those who are willing to dedicate themselves to this form of living. As we know, simplicity is the key to a happy life, a diet as simple as Bright Line Eating is the key to a happy, thin, and free life.

Made in the USA
San Bernardino, CA
03 January 2019